Eighteen brand-new
story books—exclusively
designed for this series
—guaranteed to make reading fun.

Walt Disney FUN-TO-READ LIBRARY VOLUME 1
MICKEY
MEETS THE GIANT
A Walt Disney Beginning Reader

Walt Disney FUN-TO-READ LIBRARY VOLUME 2
THUMPER'S
LITTLE SISTERS
A Walt Disn...

Walt Disney FUN-TO-READ LIBRARY VOLUME 3
PINOCCHIO'S
PROMISE
CIRCUS
A Walt Disney Beginning Reader

Disney FUN-TO-READ LIBRARY VOLUME 5
POOH'S
NEW CLOTHES
Walt Disney Beginning Reader

Walt Disney FUN-TO-READ LIBRARY VOLUME 4
GOOFY'S
BIG RACE
Beginning...

Walt Disney FUN-TO-READ LIBRARY VOLUME 6
THE UGLY
STEPSISTER
A Walt Disney Beginning Read...

Walt Disney FUN-TO-READ LIBRARY VOLUME 7
MICKEY
FINDS A KITTEN
A Walt Disney Beginning Reader

Walt Disney FUN-TO-READ LIBRARY VOLUME 8
DUMBO
AT BAT
A Walt Disney Beginning Reader

Walt Disney FUN-TO-READ LIBRARY VOLUME 9
WENDY'S
ADVENTURE IN NEVER LAND
A Walt Disney Beginning Reader

WALT

FUN-TO-READ LIBRARY

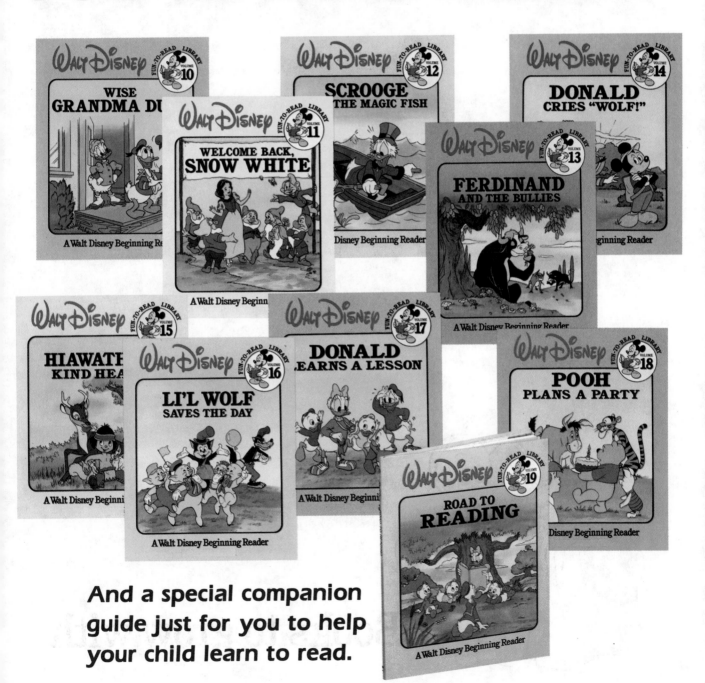

And a special companion guide just for you to help your child learn to read.

Books to grow with

Walt Disney

VOLUME 19

ROAD TO READING

WALT DISNEY FUN-TO-READ LIBRARY

ISBN 1-885222-31-9
Advance Publishers Inc., P.O. Box 2607, Winter Park, FL. 32790
Printed in the United States of America
098765432

Dear Parent,

The ability to read is the single most important gift you can give your child. But making reading fun is a real challenge.

To help you meet this challenge, Walt Disney Studios has created an 18-volume library of enchanting stories that will allow you to help your child become a successful reader.

Each story contains favorite Disney characters and has been carefully written to reinforce basic reading concepts. In addition, this indispensable parents' guide to your Beginning Reader Library explains how to identify for your child the reading concepts woven into each story.

We are sure that this series will convince your child that reading really is fun when the books are Fun-To-Read.

Sincerely,

Jodie Satterfield

Jodie Satterfield
Publisher

Giving Your Child a Good Start in Reading

Every day we are confronted with situations involving reading. From street signs to menus, from newspapers to job applications, we need the ability to unlock and understand the printed word. It is never too early to begin to develop this ability.

Educators term the period of getting ready to read, "Reading Readiness." During the earliest readiness stages, young children use all their senses to become familiar with people, places, things, and events in their world. They learn to name and describe these concepts using oral language. They learn to classify objects and ideas and think about their placement in space and time. During later readiness stages, children begin to recognize that their spoken sounds and words can be associated with the letters and words on signs and food packages and in books that have been read to them.

The period of "Beginning Reading" starts with the actual process of learning to recognize printed words and derive meaning from them. Early readers must learn to decode those funny squiggles on the page so that they can say the words, aloud or to themselves. This can be accomplished in two ways.

A *phonics* method works well with regular words, i.e., with words that follow the common rules of sound–symbol relations. For example, if your child learns the most frequently used sounds of the letters *b*, *i*, and *g*, he or she can blend those sounds together to pronounce *big*.

It is more efficient to treat irregular words, or words that don't follow the rules, as *sight words*. Thus, words such as *eight* and *rough* are easier to memorize than they are to make up elaborate rules for.

The act of deriving meaning from printed material is referred to as *comprehension*. Several skills make up this important aspect of reading. First, the child must have a working understanding of many words, phrases, and sentences, learned through listening and speaking. Then he or she must be able to relate these meanings to new situations. Learning to interpret pictures, recall details of a story, summarize the main ideas, make inferences, and draw logical conclusions are all part of building reading comprehension.

Using the Guide

The following pages of this parents' guide will familiarize you with all 18 children's books in the Walt Disney Fun-to-Read Library and give you helpful hints for using the books with your child. The books are discussed in numerical order, and each book has its own two-page spread. First you will find colorful sample pages from each of the volumes. This is followed by a brief description of the book and a list of the skills it teaches.

Next you will find a section filled with ideas for reading the book with your child, developing specific reading skills, and extending your child's understanding and enjoyment of the stories through games and activities. Each suggestion has an educational purpose, but its final selection was made because each one has proved to work and to be fun for lots of children.

Bonus Activities

Here are two fun games you can play with your child to help prepare her or him for getting more enjoyment and understanding from reading all of the volumes in the Walt Disney Fun-to-Read Library.

Alphabet Soup This game will help your child become more familiar with the letters of the alphabet. From magazines, cut out a variety of vegetable pictures totaling 26 pictures in all. Help your child write a capital letter on one side of each picture and the matching lowercase letter on the other side. Mix the letters in a paper bag or cardboard box, which will be the soup kettle. Take turns choosing a picture and naming the letter. For an older child, you may want to have him or her think of a word that begins with that letter. Later you may withdraw several letters and try to arrange them to make words.

Body Language In order to read through a story, your child must move her or his eyes from left to right across each line of print, going from the top of the page to the bottom. Use this activity to develop understanding of positional terms. Help your child identify his or her left and right hands. Place a distinguishing ring, bracelet, or bandage on the hand your child uses for eating or writing. Then have your child identify the top and bottom of the book. Finally, have your child locate these four positions on various pages of the book.

MICKEY MEETS THE GIANT

"You mean you are not afraid of me?" asked the giant.

"Afraid of you? Why, I am here to challenge you," said Mickey.

"Ho, ho, ho!" thundered the giant. "Bigger men than you have tried to beat me. They have failed. I'll just have to show you how strong I am!

Mickey Meets the Giant (Volume 1) retells the age-old story of the woodsman and the giant. When the wicked giant torments the citizens of Cedar Grove, brave Mickey comes to the rescue. This story will help your child:

—understand the concept of bravery.

—recognize the difference between real and make-believe stories.

—associate the /m/ sound with the letter *m*.

—learn the meanings of size words.

Reading *Mickey Meets the Giant*

Reading to Your Younger Child First read through the story with your child and together enjoy the way Mickey outwits the giant. Pause to discuss what is happening in the pictures. On successive readings, talk about the way characters in the story feel and how the pictures show feelings. Focus especially on Mickey's changing expressions. Emphasize that being brave sometimes means taking action, even though it is a little scary to do so.

Your Beginning Reader Reads to You Encourage your child to leaf through the book, looking at the pictures, to get a general idea of the story. Then listen attentively as your child reads to you, page by page. The first time through tell your child the unknown words so you can enjoy the full story together. On later readings, supply the irregular, or harder, words and help your child sound out the easier, more regular, ones. Discuss the pictures and the feelings in the story as suggested above.

Developing Reading Skills

Building Comprehension

After you and your child have read the story, ask questions to aid the recall of facts:

1. How did the giant scare the people?
2. How did Mickey get the giant to move the big boulder?
3. What finally convinced the giant to leave Cedar Grove?

Point out that this is a make-believe story since the events could not really happen. Explain that many make-believe stories start with the words "Once upon a time . . ."

Fun with Phonics

Read the following list of words, emphasizing the beginning /m/ sound:

Mickey   meets   make   money   must

Have your child repeat the words with you. Find the words in the book title and on the first pages. Point to the *M* or *m* at the beginning of each word and explain that the letter *m* has the "mmm" sound. Look for words in the book that begin with *m: many, man, much, made, more, miles, me.* Ask your child to think of other words that begin with *m*.

Next help your child find words that have the /m/ sound at the end: *him, from, Tom, am. Time, came, home,* and *became* also belong to this group since the final *e* is silent.

Finally, help your child find words with the /m/ sound in the middle: *sweet-smelling, woman, someone, animals, rumbling.*

Fun-to-Read Activities

Dramatization To reinforce vocabulary and comprehension of the story, have your child imitate Mickey, the giant, and the other characters. Ask him or her to show you, for example, how the characters might walk, shiver, laugh, or whistle.

Art Project and Expanding Vocabulary Have your child draw pictures of Mickey and the giant emphasizing the differences in their size. Write the size words *little, small, tiny,* and *short* on the picture of Mickey. Write the size words *big, large, huge,* and *tall* on the picture of the giant. Some children will have fun adding longer words such as *teeny-tiny, itty-bitty, gigantic,* and *super-colossal.*

Fun-to-Read Library

For more Mickey Mouse adventures, read *Mickey Finds a Kitten* (Volume 7) and *Donald Cries "Wolf!"* (Volume 14). Bravery is also a theme in *Thumper's Little Sisters* (Volume 2), *Dumbo at Bat* (Volume 8), and *Ferdinand and the Bullies* (Volume 13).

THUMPER'S LITTLE SISTERS

At last the sisters were old enough to play outside <u>all</u> day. And who did they want to play with? Thumper, of course!

"Watch out for them, Thumper," said his mother. "Don't let them get hurt."

Thumper did not want to watch out for his sisters. He wanted to play by himself. He turned his back and climbed a fence. His sisters ran across the field.

Thumper's Little Sisters (Volume 2) explores Thumper's feelings when three baby sisters arrive in his family. After a series of exciting misadventures, Thumper learns that his parents still love him and always will! This story will help your child:

—think about the importance of working together in a family.

—retell a story in time-order sequence.

—add family words to the reading vocabulary.

—associate the /t/ sound with the letter *t* and two sounds with the letters *th*.

Reading *Thumper's Little Sisters*

Reading to Your Younger Child Reading straight through the book, pause to point out action highlights in the pictures. Then read it again, more slowly. Talk about how Thumper feels at various times, and how the sisters feel. Ask if your child has ever felt like that. Point out that it is natural to feel a little hurt, or jealous, when parents pay attention to brothers or sisters, but that parents care for all their children even if it doesn't always seem that way to a child.

Your Beginning Reader Reads to You After your child examines the book to get an idea of what it is about, have her or him read it to you page by page. Be patient, encouraging your child first to read the sentences silently and ask for help with unknown words. This will build confidence for reading aloud. Talk about the pictures to keep interest lively. If your child shows signs of tiring, take a turn reading to her or him. The new reader will, of course, need more support than a more experienced reader will.

Developing Reading Skills

Building Comprehension

Encourage your child to retell the story, first to you and then to others. Emphasize getting the events in the correct time-order sequence. You may wish to use prompts such as, "How did the story begin?" "What did Thumper do next?" "Then what happened?" "How did the story end?" Reread portions of the story to clarify any confusion.

Expanding Vocabulary

Help your child recognize family words—*father, mother, baby, sister*—in the story and start a collection of "Words I Can Read" by writing the words on index cards. Spread the cards out, ask your child to find a specific word, or point to one and ask your child to read it. Ask what family words are missing—*brother, grandmother, grandfather, uncle, aunt, cousin*. Add them to the collection.

Fun with Phonics

Use the following words to emphasize that words beginning with the letter *t* all start with the /t/ sound:

time   two   tug   tree   tried

Help your child think of other words that begin with the /t/ sound.

Point out that the letters *t* and *h* used together have two very special sounds. First, listen to the sound at the beginning of these words:

Thumper   things   third   thought

Explain that you blow air between your teeth when you say these words. You make a deeper sound in your throat when you say:

they   this   that   them   there

Fun-to-Read Activities

Dramatization Ask your child to hop like Thumper and then like his little sisters. (Since Thumper is older and heavier, he makes a louder thump when he hops.)

Family Portraits Paper plates make fine frames for family portraits. Have your child paint or color Thumper's family or your own, either on the plates or on paper that is then cut out and pasted in the "frames."

Fun-to-Read Library

For another story about jealousy, read *The Ugly Stepsisters* (Volume 6). For jealousy of another type, read *Mickey Finds a Kitten* (Volume 7). After discussing Thumper's bravery in helping his sisters escape from the dog, you may want to read these books that also emphasize bravery: *Mickey Meets the Giant*, (Volume 1), *Dumbo at Bat* (Volume 8), and *Ferdinand and the Bullies* (Volume 13).

PINOCCHIO'S PROMISE

"Take this clock to Mrs. Romano. Then come home as fast as you can. Promise?"
"I promise!" said Pinocchio.

He took the clock and skipped away. Pinocchio did not see Gideon and Foulfellow. But they saw him—and the clock.

Poor Pinocchio! In *Pinocchio's Promise* (Volume 3), this wooden-headed puppet yields to temptation, much to his sorrow. Jiminy Cricket turns up just in time to save his friend from letting Geppetto down. This story will help your child:

—make inferences from pictures and text.

—learn the importance of keeping promises.

—understand that the /j/ sound may be spelled with the letter *j* or the letter *g*.

—associate the /p/ sound with the letter *p*.

Reading *Pinocchio's Promise*

Reading to Your Younger Child Before you read the story, leaf through the book with your child and talk about what might be happening in the pictures. Help your child use the characters' facial expressions and body positions as clues. Then read the story and discuss whether your child guessed correctly (made the correct inferences).

During later readings of the book, focus on Pinocchio's behavior and talk about the consequences of forgetting his promise.

Your Beginning Reader Reads to You Take turns reading through the book with your child. Pause frequently to ask your child what he or she thinks will happen next. Help her or him to look for clues in the pictures and in the words. After the story is completed, ask whether Pinocchio acted as he should have after he promised Geppetto that he would deliver the cuckoo clock. Ask your child what he or she would have done.

Developing Reading Skills

Building Comprehension

Ask questions such as the following to help your child use picture and context clues to make inferences about the characters' actions:

1. Why did Foulfellow pick up the two old circus tickets? How did he use them to trick Pinocchio?
2. Why did Pinocchio run from the ticket man?
3. Why did the lion begin to purr?
4. How do you think Pinocchio felt when Geppetto told him that he had planned to take Pinocchio to the circus?

Expanding Vocabulary

Help your child find the following circus words in the story: *circus, ticket, tent, elephant, clown, horse, strong man, lion, ring, ringmaster*. Write each word on an index card and help your child draw the appropriate picture on the back. Point to one of the words and ask your child to read it. If help is needed, your child can turn the card over to "read" the picture.

Spelling Hints for Better Readers

Say the following words and ask your child what they have in common: *Jiminy, just,* and *jumped*. (They all begin with the /j/ sound.) Show that they begin with the letter *J* or *j*. Next say the words *Geppetto* and *gently*. Help your child recognize that these words also start with the /j/ sound. Show that they begin with the letter *G* or *g*. Explain that there are two common ways to spell the /j/ sound—with a *j* or a *g*. Finally, say the words *Pinocchio* and *promise*. Show that these words begin with the letter *P* or *p*.

Fun-to-Read Activities

Art Project Provide a big piece of paper and help your child make a circus poster. Encourage your child to include all the circus characters and animals Pinocchio encountered in the story. Print labels on the pictures.

Circus Party You may want to help your child plan a costume party for little friends. Make clown hats for the guests and serve popcorn. Read *Pinocchio's Promise* to the group and have them act out favorite scenes.

Fun-to-Read Library

Your child will find it fun to compare how Pinocchio was tricked with how Pooh and his friends were tricked in *Pooh's New Clothes* (Volume 5). For another circus story, read *Dumbo at Bat* (Volume 8).

GOOFY'S BIG RACE

"Last one to Horner's Corners is a slowpoke!" Donald called.
He drove away fast. *Va-ROOOM!*

Goofy blew his horn. *Ah-OOOO-gah!* "Come on, Bessie," he said. "Slow and steady, steady and slow. That's the way we always go." And away he drove. *Chug-a-chug-chug.*

HORNER'S CORNERS 15 MI.

Everybody likes to win. In *Goofy's Big Race* (Volume 4), your child will learn that you don't always have to be the fastest to win. This story will help your child:

— understand the importance of determination.

— develop an awareness of the sequence of events.

— become familiar with words that have opposite meanings (antonyms).

— associate the /g/ sound with the letter *g*.

Reading *Goofy's Big Race*

Reading to Your Younger Child As you read the book with your child, point out the differences between Goofy's car and Donald's. On successive readings talk about Goofy's determination, and how Donald's overconfidence cost him the race.

Your Beginning Reader Reads to You Have your child look at the pictures to get an idea of the story. Then listen as your child reads to you. Pause where appropriate to have your child guess what might happen next. Then continue reading to see what actually does happen. Help your child with unknown words. On successive readings, encourage your child to sound out the easier words. Supply only the irregular words. Discuss the importance of determination and doing one's best.

Developing Reading Skills

Building Comprehension

After you and your child have read the story, ask questions such as these to aid his or her recall of the events:
1. What did Donald ask Goofy to do? Why?
2. Where did Donald stop first? Why? What happened next?
3. What other things happened to Donald?
4. Who was Bessie? Why do you think Goofy won the race? Why is it important to keep going?

Explain that thinking about what happens first, next, and last in a story can lead to better understanding.

Expanding Vocabulary

Read these pairs of words to your child:

up/down   go/stop
slow/fast   wet/dry

Explain that the words in each pair have opposite meanings. They are called **antonyms.** Have your child recall when these words were used in the story. Your child may enjoy making a book of opposites. Other words can be added as other stories are read.

Fun with Phonics

Read the following words, emphasizing the beginning /g/ sound:

Goofy   good   go

Have your child repeat the words with you. Find the words on the first pages and read them again. Point to the *G* or *g* at the beginning of each of the words, explaining that this is one sound for the letter *g.* These words have the /g/ sound. Look for other words in the book that begin with *g: game, get, got, going.* Ask your child to think of words not in the book that also begin with the letter *g.*

Fun-to-Read Activities

Dramatization Use toy cars to act out the race. Allow your child to take turns being Goofy and Donald. Discuss how each one felt when he had won or lost.

Transportation Words Have your child draw pictures to illustrate each of the transportation words in the story. Write *car, bike, truck,* and *train* under each of the drawings. Your child may wish to draw and label pictures of other transportation words as well.

Fun-to-Read Library

For other kinds of races, read *Li'l Wolf Saves the Day* (Volume 16) and *Donald Learns a Lesson* (Volume 17). For another story about determination, read *Dumbo at Bat* (Volume 8). Follow Donald's crazy adventures in *Wise Grandma Duck* (Volume 10) and *Donald Cries "Wolf!"* (Volume 14). To show that Donald can sometimes be wise, refer to *Scrooge and the Magic Fish* (Volume 12).

POOH'S NEW CLOTHES

"I can make these clothes for you," said Sly Fox. "I have some of the best cloth ever made. No other cloth is as soft, as smooth, or as light. It is also magic cloth. Only <u>wise</u> people can see it."

"My word," muttered Owl.

"How wonderful," said Rabbit.

In *Pooh's New Clothes* (Volume 5), Sly Fox sets up his tailor shop in the Hundred Acre Wood to make a suit for Pooh out of "magic" cloth. According to Sly, the cloth is magic because only wise people can see it. This story will help your child:

—use pictures to interpret a story.

—recognize the importance of trusting one's own judgment.

—associate the /p/ sound with the letter *p*, the /b/ sound with the letter *b*, and the /r/ sound with the letter *r*.

—learn words for clothing.

Reading *Pooh's New Clothes*

Reading to Your Younger Child First read the entire story. Pause long enough to discuss the pictures. Ask your child if he or she can see the magic cloth. On successive readings, discuss how Pooh and his friends felt when they couldn't see the magic cloth and why they said they could see it. Emphasize the importance of relying on what you can see with your own eyes.

Your Beginning Reader Reads to You Have your child look through the pages of the book, paying particular attention to the pictures. Ask your child if there is anything unusual in any of the pictures. Then listen carefully as your child reads to you. The first time through, supply difficult or unknown words. On later readings, encourage your child to sound out words and look for clues within the sentences. The pictures may also offer clues to words. Discuss the feelings of Pooh and his friends as suggested above.

Developing Reading Skills

Building Comprehension

After you and your child have read the story, ask questions such as these:
1. Why did Pooh and his friends think Sly Fox must be important?
2. What did Sly Fox promise to do? What did he want in return?
3. Who knew Sly Fox was a trickster?
4. If you couldn't see the clothes, what would you say? Why is it a good idea to trust your own judgment?

Point out that pictures can be excellent clues. Ask your child which pictures helped him or her to know that the magic cloth was not real.

Fun with Phonics

Review the sound of the letter *p*. Read each group of words. Have your child repeat only those words that begin with the /p/ sound.
- a) party, clothes, Piglet
- b) pants, Pooh, Fox
- c) honey, pretty, magic
- d) trick, tree, place

Introduce the /b/ sound. Read these words:
bear   birthday   beautiful   better
Ask your child to repeat the words with you. Explain that each word begins with the letter *b*. Look for other words in the story that begin with *b: but, bee, brain, brave, big, best, by, beginning, believe*. Encourage your child to think of other words that begin with *b*.

Next introduce the /r/ sound for the letter *r*. Read these words:
Roo   Robin   Rabbit
Ask your child to repeat the words with you. Explain that each word begins with *r*. Look for other words in the story: *remembered, really, right, real, run*. Think of others.

Fun-to-Read Activities

Clothing Word Cards Help your child recall the clothing words that appeared in the story: *suit, shirt, outfit, pants, jacket, cloth*. Cut out pictures from magazines that illustrate these and other clothing words. Glue each to an index card. Write the word for each article of clothing on another card. You and your child can play a matching game with the cards.

Fun-to-Read Library

Compare how Pooh and his friends were tricked with how Pinocchio was tricked in *Pinocchio's Promise* (Volume 3). For other stories about being wise, read *Wise Grandma Duck* (Volume 10) and *Scrooge and the Magic Fish* (Volume 12).

THE UGLY STEPSISTERS

"Stepmother! Drizella and Anastasia! I am so happy to see you!" said Cinderella.

"My, Cinderella—how pretty you look," said the stepmother. "Would you send our clothes up right away? The girls must have their beauty rest. We've had a busy day."

"Yes, Stepmother—whatever you say," said Cinderella.

"Oh, boy! Look at all those boxes. It looks as if they are going to stay a long time," Jaq said to Gus. Then they hurried after Cinderella to see if they could help.

In *The Ugly Stepsisters* (Volume 6), Cinderella and Prince Charming decide to have a surprise party for some very important people. But Cinderella's stepmother and stepsisters have a surprise of their own for Cinderella. This story will help your child:

—recognize contrasts in pictures and in words.

—understand how jealousy can cause trouble.

—learn more about words that have opposite meanings (antonyms).

—associate the /s/ sound with the letter *s*.

Reading *The Ugly Stepsisters*

Reading to Your Younger Child When you introduce the book, read through with your child and see how Cinderella's stepsisters are surprised in the end. Pause to point out and discuss how the pictures show the contrasts between Cinderella and her stepsisters. On successive readings, spend more time talking about feelings of jealousy, contrasting these with feelings of love and kindness.

Your Beginning Reader Reads to You Have your child look at the pictures to get an idea of the story. Encourage your child to point out contrasts between Cinderella and her stepsisters as you look at the pictures. Then listen as your child reads to you. Help with unknown words so you can enjoy the story together. On later readings, encourage your child to sound out unknown words and use sentence and picture clues. Discuss the pictures and the feelings of the characters. Focus on the contrast between the loving and kind Cinderella and the jealous and mean stepsisters.

Developing Reading Skills

Building Comprehension

When you and your child have finished reading the story, ask questions such as the following to aid his or her recall of facts:

1. How did the stepsisters act toward Cinderella? Why?
2. How did Cinderella treat her stepsisters? How do you feel when you have to be nice to someone who isn't very nice to you?
3. How did the mice Jaq and Gus help?
4. How do you think the stepsisters felt after learning the party was for them?

Point out to your child how pictures and words can help show contrasts in a story.

Expanding Vocabulary

Have your child listen to these pairs of words:
kind/mean   nice/wicked   laugh/cry
beautiful/ugly   happy/sad

Point out that the words in each pair have opposite meanings. They are called **antonyms.** Discuss how the words describe the characters in the story. Your child can add these pairs of words to the book of opposites suggested earlier for *Goofy's Big Race* (Volume 4).

Fun with Phonics

Read the following list of words, emphasizing the /s/ sound at the beginning of each:
stepsisters   servant   salt   surprise

Have your child repeat the words with you. Find *Stepsisters* in the title, pointing to the *S* at the beginning of the word. Explain that the letter *s* has the /s/ sound. Find other words in the story that begin with the /s/ sound: *stepmother, said, sang, some, soon.* Look for words that contain the /s/ sound either in the middle or at the end.

Fun-to-Read Activities

Dramatization Discuss with your child how the characters acted in each situation. Then have your child dramatize the following scenes:
—Cinderella greeting her stepsisters
—the stepsisters eavesdropping as Cinderella plans the party
—the reactions of the guests to the stepsisters in their nightgowns

Fun-to-Read Library

For other kinds of parties, read *Wendy's Adventure in Never Land* (Volume 9), *Wise Grandma Duck* (Volume 10), and *Pooh Plans a Party* (Volume 18). Jealousy of another sort is described in *Thumper's Little Sisters* (Volume 2) and *Mickey Finds a Kitten* (Volume 7).

MICKEY FINDS A KITTEN

"But that isn't true," said Morty. "Pluto is a great <u>dog</u>. Remember when we were little, Pluto?"

"You were the best baby-sitter we ever had," said Ferdie.

"You are still the best watchdog," said Minnie. "I am never afraid when you are nearby."

"Pluto," Mickey said, "we are best friends! Nobody can ever take your place with me."

Pluto grinned. He wagged his tail.

In *Mickey Finds a Kitten* (Volume 7), a foundling kitten becomes the focus of Mickey's attention. Pluto, puzzled by this shift of Mickey's affection, tries everything to regain Mickey's love, including acting like a kitten. This story will help your child:

—make inferences from pictures.

—appreciate his or her own special qualities.

—associate the /k/ sound with the letters *c* and *k*.

—learn words for items in the home.

Reading *Mickey Finds a Kitten*

Reading to Your Younger Child When you introduce the book, ask your child if he or she has ever felt ignored when someone has arrived—a new baby brother or sister or even a visiting relative. Then read the story with your child. Pause to discuss what is happening in the pictures. On successive readings, discuss how Pluto felt and why he tried to act like a kitten. Have your child find the pictures that show Pluto's feelings.

Your Beginning Reader Reads to You Encourage your child to browse through the book, paying particular attention to the pictures. Ask how Pluto seems to look in the pictures. Have your child suggest possible reasons for Pluto's expressions. Then have your child begin reading. Listen attentively and supply any unknown words so you can enjoy the entire story together. During later readings, encourage your child to sound out words and to look at surrounding words and sentences for clues. Spend more time discussing the feelings of the characters. Use the pictures to help.

Developing Reading Skills

Building Comprehension

After you and your child have read the story, ask questions such as these:
1. Why did everyone make such a fuss over the kitten?
2. How did Pluto feel about the kitten?
3. Why did Pluto start acting like a kitten?
4. How did Mickey figure out what was the matter with Pluto?
5. Do you ever act like someone other than yourself to get attention? Why? How do people react when you do this?

Fun with Phonics

Read the following list of words, emphasizing the beginning /k/ sound:

    cars   kitty   cat   cold   kitten

Have your child repeat the words with you. Then ask what sound begins each word. Read the sentence "Stay out of the way of cars, kitty cat . . ." on the fourth page of the story. Point to the *c* in *cars*, the *k* in *kitty*, and the *c* in *cat*. Explain that there is more than one way to write the /k/ sound. The letters *c* and *k* and the combination *ck* share the /k/ sound. Look for other words that begin with the /k/ sound.

Tell your child that the /k/ sound can come at the ends of words, such as in:

    walk   milk   woke   rake

Have your child repeat the words with you. Find these and others in the story. As you locate a word, point to the letter(s) that make the /k/ sound: li*k*e, wor*k*, ba*ck*, loo*k*.

Fun-to-Read Activities

Dramatization Your child may enjoy making the sounds and motions to imitate the kitten and Pluto in different parts of the story.

Art and Words Help your child draw an empty room on construction paper. In old magazines, find pictures of furniture and arrange them in the room. Help glue them in place and label them. Your child may enjoy making different rooms in a house or apartment.

Field Trip Take your child to a pet shop. Ask the proprietor how to care for a kitten or a puppy. Discuss other pets, where they live, what they eat, what toys they play with.

Fun-to-Read Library

Compare Pluto's feelings with Thumper's feelings in *Thumper's Little Sisters* (Volume 2). Read more about Mickey in *Mickey Meets the Giant* (Volume 1) and *Donald Cries "Wolf!"* (Volume 14).

DUMBO AT BAT

Now the game was up to Dumbo.
The pitcher threw the ball.
"Strike one!" called the ringmaster.
The pitcher threw the ball again.
Dumbo swung, but his ears got in the way of the bat.
"Strike two!" called the ringmaster.

Timothy ran to Dumbo. He tied up his friend's ears. Then he whispered once again, "Believe, Dumbo! Believe!"

When the circus shuts down for a few days, the clowns and the animals have a big baseball game in *Dumbo at Bat* (Volume 8). But Dumbo doesn't know how to play baseball—yet! This story will help your child:

—recognize the importance of self-confidence.

—distinguish between real and make-believe.

—learn action words.

—associate the /d/ sound with the letter *d* and the /b/ sound with the letter *b*.

Reading *Dumbo at Bat*

Reading to Your Younger Child First read through to the end so you and your child can enjoy the excitement of the big game. Pause to look at what is happening in the pictures. On successive readings, use the pictures to discuss how Dumbo's feelings change. Focus on how Dumbo gains self-confidence.

Your Beginning Reader Reads to You Ask your child to think about the very first time he or she had to do something in front of people. As your child browses through the book, explain that Dumbo is about to have a similar experience. Listen as your child reads to you and supply the unknown words. On later readings, encourage your child to sound out words and to use the pictures for clues. Use the pictures to discuss how and why Dumbo's feelings change in the end.

Developing Reading Skills

Building Comprehension

When you and your child have read the story, ask questions to aid the recall of facts:
1. Who was on each of the teams? Name the members of Dumbo's team.
2. How did they get ready for the game?
3. What did Dumbo's team think of his playing? How did that make Dumbo feel?
4. What did Timothy tell Dumbo? Did it help?
5. What lesson can you learn about believing in yourself?

Point out to your child that this story is make-believe. Some parts could happen, but you would never see animals playing baseball.

Expanding Vocabulary

Read these words to your child:
throw hit catch run play practice
Ask your child to think about what kind of words these are. Explain that they describe actions. As you read the story, find these and other action words with your child, who may enjoy making cards with the word on one side

and, on the other side, a picture that shows what the word means.

Fun with Phonics

Read the following list of words, emphasizing the beginning /d/ sound:

delight Dumbo day down do don't did
Have your child repeat the words with you. Then ask your child to say just the beginning sound of the words. Explain that each word begins with the letter *d*. Find the words *Dumbo* and *delight* on the first page, pointing to the letter *D* or *d* in each word. Think of other words that begin with *d*.

Next, review the /b/ sound. Find the word *Bat* in the title. Point to the *B* as you say the word. Read each group of words below. Have your child listen to the words and repeat only those that begin with the /b/ sound:

a) bat, baseball, down
b) day, don't, believe
c) behind, do, best
d) bear, base, ball, did, do, be

Fun-to-Read Activities

Baseball Game Take your child to a school yard or playground and explain the game. Also watch it on TV. Practice throwing, catching, batting, and running.

Field Trip Take your child to the zoo and record the animals you see. Your child can draw a picture of each animal in the story and label it with your help.

Fun-to-Read Library

Compare Dumbo's willingness to try hard with Goofy's determination in *Goofy's Big Race* (Volume 4). Read more about the circus in *Pinocchio's Promise* (Volume 3).

WENDY'S ADVENTURE IN NEVER LAND

Peter Pan was sorry to see Wendy and the boys go. But Tinker Bell sprinkled them all with pixie dust so they could not change their minds.

Then she and Peter flew them home.

Wendy tucked her sleepy brothers into bed. Then she went to the window.

"Good-bye, Peter Pan and Tinker Bell," she said. "Someday we will see you again. Even though we grow up, part of us will never really grow up all the way."

Wendy's Adventure in Never Land (Volume 9) tells the story of three children who think they never want to grow up, until they get to the place where you never grow older, where there are no birthdays —or birthday parties! This story will help your child:

—understand the concept of growing up.

—predict outcomes.

—learn the long and short /i/ sounds.

—recognize rhyming words.

Reading *Wendy's Adventure in Never Land*

Reading to Your Younger Child Before you read the book, explain to your child how one starts out as a tiny baby and grows and changes into a child, a teenager, an adult, and an elderly person. Now read the book with your child, pausing long enough to discuss what is happening in the pictures. On successive readings, discuss the feelings of the children, how they feel about not growing up, and why they would change their minds and go home. Discuss with your child what he or she would do given the opportunity to go to Never Land.

Your Beginning Reader Reads to You Ask your child what it would it be like always to be a child. Explain that the children in the book go to a place where they will never grow up. Ask your child to predict the outcome while looking through the book. Listen as your child reads and help with unknown words. On successive readings, supply only the harder words. Encourage your child to sound out easier words and to use picture and word clues.

Developing Reading Skills

Building Comprehension

When you and your child have read the story, ask questions such as these:
1. Did the story end the way you thought it would? Why?
2. Why did Wendy, John, and Michael decide to go to Never Land? Is there really such a place?
3. Why couldn't there be any birthday parties in Never Land?
4. Why were the children happy to return home?

Fun with Phonics

Explain to your child that the letter *i* can have a long sound like the *i* in *Michael* or a short sound like the *i* in *pillow*. Find the words *Michael* and *pillow* on the first page and point to the *i* in each.

Read the words below with the long /i/ sound. Have your child repeat them:

fight   I   idea   right   night   cries   like

Then read these words with the short /i/ sound. Have your child repeat:

in   if   it   is   him   window   quickly   give

Mix words from the two groups. Have your child tell you if the word has the long /i/ sound or the short /i/ sound.

Rhyming Words Read each group of rhyming words. Have your child repeat the words. Ask how they sound the same.

fight and *right* and *night*   *Hook* and *look*
Smee and *see* and *tree*   *John* and *gone*
door and *floor*   *grow* and *row* and *go*

Think of other words that rhyme. Your child may enjoy making up rhymes using these and other rhyming words. Find the rhyming words in *Goofy's Big Race* (Volume 4).

Fun-to-Read Activities

Dramatization Encourage your child to choose one of the characters from the story and think about how that character would act. Then have your child act out the part. Your child may enjoy using a prop or wearing a costume.

Fun-to-Read Library

Read about another birthday party in *Pooh Plans a Party* (Volume 18) and about how Thumper and his baby sisters grow up in *Thumper's Little Sisters* (Volume 2).

WISE GRANDMA DUCK

Donald grabbed the cover from the plate. "But, but—" he sputtered.

"It's medicine!" said Louie. "It's for headaches, stomachaches, and sore muscles!"

Huey, Dewey, and Louie couldn't stop laughing.

"I hope you are happy, Donald, dear," Grandma said. "I wanted each of you to have what you worked for."

Then she laughed, too. And for once in his life, Donald Duck could not think of a thing to say.

Wise Grandma Duck (Volume 10) parallels the story of the wise little hen. As the nephews, Huey, Dewey, and Louie, work hard to help Grandma Duck on her farm, Donald resorts to trickery to avoid labor. At the tale's end, each character receives his earned reward. This story will help your child:

—realize the value of helping others.

—appreciate the traits of cooperation and industriousness in contrast to self-indulgence and laziness.

—associate the letter *f* with the /f/ sound.

—add food words to the reading vocabulary.

Reading *Wise Grandma Duck*

Reading to Your Younger Child Read the story with your child and help describe the illustrated chores. As you reread the story, pause to discuss the characters' actions and feelings. Ask your child to point out clues that Donald was not as sick as he claimed. Emphasize the helpfulness displayed by Huey, Dewey, and Louie.

Your Beginning Reader Reads to You You may wish to give your child some time alone with the book, allowing him or her to become familiar with the pictures and the general plot of the story. As your child reads to you, pay careful attention so that you may quickly supply any unfamiliar words and you can both enjoy the continuity of the tale. As you listen to the story on other occasions, ask your child to sound out the harder words on his or her own and offer help only after a sincere effort has been made. Discuss the characters and illustrations as mentioned above.

Developing Reading Skills

Building Comprehension

After you and your child have read *Wise Grandma Duck*, use questions such as those below to help your child recall pertinent facts about the story:
1. Who helped Grandma Duck do her chores? What were these chores?
2. What reward did each nephew get? What reward did Donald get?
3. Were the rewards fair? Why or why not?

You may want to help your child recall incidents where he or she earned rewards by helping somebody else. It may be interesting to ask your child to select a reward for someone who helped her or him.

Fun with Phonics

Read aloud the following list of words, paying special attention to the beginning /f/ sound:

farm   fresh   food

Have your child say each word with you. Find the words on the first pages and say them again. Point out that these words all begin with the letter *f*. Look through the story together to find other words that begin with *f*. They include *fun, feeling, firewood, fell, fishing, for, find, faster,* and *fine.* Challenge your child to think of other words that begin with the /f/ sound.

Fun-to-Read Activities

Dramatization Your child will delight in mimicking Donald with a sore arm or a backache, and telling Grandma why he can't work that day. Then have your child show how Huey, Dewey, or Louie would act if Grandma asked them to do something.

Favorite Foods Ask your child to recall words from the story that suggest food. These can be general words such as *breakfast, supper,* and *dinner,* or specific words such as *lemonade, apples, cookies, corn, pumpkins, pie,* and *cream.* Write each word on a sheet of notebook paper. Have your child draw a picture of each item on the paper, or cut pictures from magazines and paste them on the correct sheets of paper. Many children will wish to continue this activity by adding other favorite food words to the collection. They may want to use colored paper to make a cover for a bound booklet of the papers.

Fun-to-Read Library

For more Donald Duck stories, read *Goofy's Big Race* (Volume 4), *Donald Cries "Wolf!"* (Volume 14), and *Donald Learns a Lesson* (Volume 17). For another story about cooperation, read *Welcome Back, Snow White* (Volume 11).

WELCOME BACK, SNOW WHITE

All the dwarfs ran outside. Even Bashful came and stood shyly behind Doc. Everyone waited for the carriage to stop. Out of the carriage stepped the beautiful Snow White.

"Welcome back, Snow White," sang the Seven Dwarfs.

Snow White looked just like a princess. Her sweet smile, her gentle hands, and the love in her eyes were the same as ever.

Imagine how excited the Seven Dwarfs are when they learn that their beloved friend is coming for a visit! *Welcome Back, Snow White* (Volume 11) shows how they prepare for the visit. After a scrambled start, they find that working together is the best method. This story will help your child:

—use picture clues and descriptions to identify characters in the story.

—learn the importance of teamwork.

—explore words with opposite meanings (antonyms).

—associate the short /u/ sound with the letter *u*.

Reading *Welcome Back, Snow White*

Reading to Your Younger Child As you read, help your child decide which dwarf is which in the pictures—for example, Happy has a smile on his face and Grumpy wears a perpetual frown. You might ask how Sleepy and Sneezy got their names. Comment on the messy state of the dwarfs' house in the beginning and praise them for cleaning it. Discuss how the cleanup went faster after the dwarfs began to cooperate.

Your Beginning Reader Reads to You Before your child begins to read the story, it may be helpful to identify each dwarf and write his name on a piece of paper. Point out ways to remember the names. For example, Doc and Dopey begin with the same letter, as do Sleepy and Sneezy. Doc has the shortest name and Bashful the longest.

As your child reads the story, discuss how the dwarfs feel and what they do to get ready for Snow White's visit. Emphasize that working together according to a plan makes the chores easier for one and all.

Developing Reading Skills

Building Comprehension

Help your child understand the dwarfs' actions by asking questions such as the following:

1. Was Sleepy very helpful in the beginning? How did he keep awake later?
2. What happened when Dopey couldn't figure out what to do with the dust?
3. How did Doc solve the problems that the dwarfs were having in cleaning the cottage?
4. Do you think Snow White was surprised to see everything so clean? How did the dwarfs feel when she was so pleased?

Expanding Vocabulary

Write each pair of words shown at the top of the next column on an index card. Talk about the meanings of the words and point out that the words in each pair are opposites. Cut the

cards in two so one word is on each piece. Have your child reassemble the puzzle pieces.

old/new   clean/dirty   happy/sad
wet/dry   messy/neat

Fun with Phonics

Help your child read the following words: *up, us, upside, until, unhappy.* Have him or her listen to the sound of the beginning letter *u.* Explain that this is called a short /u/ sound. Challenge advanced readers to think of words that have this sound in the middle. The following examples are taken from the story: *hug, just, jump, must, Grumpy, Humph, dust.*

Fun-to-Read Activities

Dramatization Your child and his or her friends will have a great time pretending to be the various dwarfs. They may enjoy taking turns and having the other children guess which dwarf was imitated.

Chore Time Encourage your child to help with chores around the house. Making a list or chart of jobs to be done and then crossing them off as they are completed gives a child a great sense of accomplishment.

Fun-to-Read Library

Another delightful story about working together is *Wise Grandma Duck* (Volume 10).

SCROOGE AND THE MAGIC FISH

Uncle Scrooge went home. His palace was gone. So were his throne and his crown. All that was left was a sad Donald Duck.

"I don't know what happened, Uncle Scrooge," said Donald. "All of a sudden the palace was gone. And now the money bin is half-empty again."

Uncle Scrooge began to cry. He cried for his gold crown and his lost kingdom. He cried for the heaps of money that had disappeared.

"I am only a poor old duck once again!" he sobbed.

Scrooge and the Magic Fish (Volume 12) retells the age-old tale of the fisherman and his wife but places the action in a more familiar setting. Scrooge McDuck demands more and more from the magic fish and finally receives a just reward for his greed. This story will help your child:

—recognize and evaluate the consequences of acting greedily.

—add nautical terms to the reading vocabulary.

—associate the letter *o* with its short and long sounds.

—learn to deal with money on a realistic level.

Reading *Scrooge and the Magic Fish*

Reading to Your Younger Child Read the story through with your child. Pause to look at pictures of particular interest, but focus on continuity during this reading. Subsequent readings can be interrupted at important points of the tale to examine the plot in greater depth. Discuss greed and help your child find evidence of Scrooge's greediness. Point out that greed only made Scrooge more and more unhappy, and that a person's happiness is not guaranteed by money.

Your Beginning Reader Reads to You Ask your child first to read the book silently, then aloud. Offer help and encouragement with unknown words. Discuss the pictures, but place emphasis on completing the story so as to preserve a sense of the sequence of events.

Developing Reading Skills

Building Comprehension

Ask your child to retell the story in the correct time order. Questions such as those below will encourage your child to think about the story on different levels.

1. Would you be happy with a half-full bin of money? What would you do with it?
2. Do you think a fish can really talk? Was the fish wise? Was Scrooge wise?
3. What would you wish for if you had three wishes? Would you be happy then?

Expanding Vocabulary

Point out nautical words in the story: *sea, harbor, deep water, boat, fishing pole, rowed.* From a large cardboard box, make a fish pond. Put fish-shaped word cards with paper clip mouths in it. To make a fishing pole, attach a magnet with a string to one end of a short stick and have your child catch one fish at a time. If he or she can read the word, the fish may be kept. If not, you sound out the word for your child and toss the fish back into the pond.

Fun with Phonics

Read these two rows of words to your child:
1. so, old, only, go
2. not, lots, off, on

Point out that the vowel sounds in both rows are spelled with the letter *o*, but that they have two entirely different sounds. Words such as *so* have a long /o/ sound that is pronounced the same as the letter itself. Words such as *not* have a short /o/ sound that is pronounced as "ah."

Find other words in the book that begin with or contain the letter *o*. Ask which of the /o/ sounds your child hears as you read each word.

Fun-to-Read Activities

Learning About Money Familiarize your child with coins and their values. Some children may be ready to distinguish the denominations of bills. Save cans, food boxes, paper bags, etc., so your child can play store with friends. When you and your child shop, have him or her help you look for the best values.

Fun-to-Read Library

Compare Donald's actions in this story with his actions in *Goofy's Big Race* (Volume 4), *Donald Cries "Wolf!"* (Volume 14), and *Donald Learns a Lesson* (Volume 17). Compare the wise fish with Christopher Robin in *Pooh's New Clothes* (Volume 5) and with Grandma Duck in *Wise Grandma Duck* (Volume 10).

FERDINAND AND THE BULLIES

Ferdinand's eyes flashed. He gave a great snort. He pawed the ground. With a mighty bellow, he ran at the bullies. He butted with his horns. He kicked with his feet.

The young bullies cried out in fear. They tried to run this way. They tried to run that way. But Ferdinand was everywhere at once. The young bullies ran away.

Ferdinand and the Bullies (Volume 13) shows how a peace-loving Spanish bull tolerates the jokes played on him by young bullies until his nephew's safety is at stake. This story will help your child:

—learn the virtue of tolerance and the purpose of anger.

—compare and contrast the actions and attitudes of Ferdinand and the bullies.

—recognize and identify new action words.

—relate the /r/ sound to the letter *r*.

Reading *Ferdinand and the Bullies*

Reading to Your Younger Child As you read *Ferdinand and the Bullies* to your child, use the illustrations to point out the differences in attitudes and actions between Ferdinand and the bulls. Show, for example, that Ferdinand spent most of his time sitting under the tree smelling flowers while the other bulls were snorting and practicing for the bullring. Discuss how the younger bulls' attitudes changed after Ferdinand got angry. You may point out that walking away from a bad situation is often the wisest and bravest thing to do.

Your Beginning Reader Reads to You Before your child reads to you allow him or her to spend a few quiet moments looking through the book. This provides a background for understanding and increases anticipation of the events in the story. During the reading assist with the correct pronunciation of difficult words. Discuss Ferdinand's reactions to the bullies' jokes. Ask your child to explain why Ferdinand waited so long before showing his strength. Discuss the wisdom of his holding his temper.

Developing Reading Skills

Building Comprehension

Help your child understand *Ferdinand and the Bullies* by posing questions:
1. Do you think Ferdinand felt angry when the first jokes were played on him? Why or why not? Why didn't Ferdinand fight back?
2. What finally made Ferdinand angry enough to fight the young bulls?
3. Do you think Ramon will be like Ferdinand when he grows up? Would you like to be like Ferdinand?
4. Do you think the bullies will play any more jokes on Ferdinand?

Expanding Vocabulary

Write the action words listed in the next column on index cards. Place the cards facedown on a table. Have your child select a card, read it aloud, and tell whether the word tells something Ferdinand often did in the story or something the bullies often did.

sit	smell	walk	sleep
bellow	snort	paw	butt
kick	sneeze	sneer	snicker

You may wish to point out that all of these action words are called verbs. They tell what someone or something does. You might want to refer to the action-word cards you made for *Dumbo at Bat* (Volume 8), to reinforce the meaning of action words.

Fun with Phonics

Read the following words to your child: *rest, Ramon, real, right*. Have her or him listen to the /r/ sound of the beginning letter *r*. Leaf through the book together and have your child search for other words that begin with *r*. Help pronounce each of these words. For children who are more advanced, point out that the *r* retains the /r/ sound in the middle of words such as *bullring*, *covered*, and *around*.

Fun-to-Read Activities

Dramatization Have your child imitate the actions of the bulls. Ask her or him to show what a bull does when it *snorts, bellows, paws the ground, butts, kicks,* and *swishes its tail*. Then ask your child to show how Ferdinand acts.

Fun-to-Read Library

You may wish to compare Ferdinand's bravery with that of the heroes in *Mickey Meets the Giant* (Volume 1) and *Thumper's Little Sisters* (Volume 2).

DONALD CRIES "WOLF!"

Mickey got down on the ground. He crawled back and forth. Then he stood up and glared at Donald. "I don't see any wolf tracks," he said. "But I do see your tracks, Donald. That was you growling like a wolf, wasn't it?"

"Listen, Mickey," Donald said. "I really wish you would—"

"No!" Mickey shouted. "I'm going back to bed. And don't you try to trick me again, Donald. I'm not going to get up—for any reason!" He went back into the tent.

Donald Cries "Wolf!" (Volume 14) provides a new setting for a favorite old fable about the boy who cried wolf. When Mickey takes him camping, Donald can't sleep. He uses devious tactics to try to get Mickey to stay up and keep him company—but his tactics backfire. This story will help your child:

- —resolve feelings of fear of being alone in the dark.
- —realize the importance of telling the truth.
- —recognize compound words in reading.
- —associate the /w/ and /wh/ sounds with the letters *w* and *wh*.

Reading *Donald Cries "Wolf!"*

Reading to Your Younger Child Before you read the story, encourage your child to leaf through the book, page by page, and tell you what he or she thinks is happening in the pictures. Then read the story and clarify any misconceptions. Talk about how Donald felt in the beginning and how he acted to get over this feeling. Did your child ever feel that way? Point out that it is not bad to feel a little lonely or scared at bedtime, but that a better way to handle the feeling is to rest quietly and think about some nice things that have happened. It also helps to tell someone how you feel.

Your Beginning Reader Reads to You Give your child time to examine the pictures and predict what the story is about. Then listen as he or she reads the text. Supply difficult words the first time through. On later readings, help your child use the illustrations, sounds of letters, and meanings of surrounding words to figure out unknown words. Discuss Donald's and your child's feelings as suggested above.

Developing Reading Skills

Building Comprehension

After reading *Donald Cries "Wolf!"*, have your child look at the pictures again and retell the story in her or his own words. Then close the book and challenge your child to name all the animals Donald saw in the woods (skunk, owl, rabbit, raccoons, wolf). Ask what kinds of sounds these animals made.

Expanding Vocabulary

This story contains four compound words:
campfire   flashlight   bedroll   something
Explain that a big word made from two little words is a compound word. For example, *camp* and *fire* are joined together to make *campfire*. Ask what little words are in the other three compound words.

Fun with Phonics

Read these words to emphasize the /w/ sound:
wild   walked   woods

Point out these words on the first two pages and show that they all begin with the letter *w*. Ask your child to suggest other words that begin with the /w/ sound; e.g., *wolf, word, wink*.

Next, write these words on a piece of paper:
what   where   when   why
Read the words, emphasizing the /wh/ sound at the beginning. Explain that the letters *w* and *h* work together to make this sound. All of the words above are question words. One other question word, *who*, has a beginning /h/ sound, so it must be learned as an exception to the rule.

Fun-to-Read Activities

Day and Night Have your child draw two pictures of the campsite, one during the daytime and one at night. Talk about what a camper might see—and hear—during both times.

Hide the Wolf Make a small picture or model of a wolf. Have your child cover his or her eyes while you "hide" the wolf in plain sight. As your child walks around the room looking for the wolf, say, "You're getting warmer" or "You're getting cooler." When the child gets "hot" and finds the wolf, it becomes her or his turn to hide the wolf.

Fun-to-Read Library

Compare Donald's actions in this story with his not-so-wise actions in *Goofy's Big Race* (Volume 4), *Wise Grandma Duck* (Volume 10), and *Donald Learns a Lesson* (Volume 17). For another story featuring a wolf, see *Li'l Wolf Saves the Day* (Volume 16).

HIAWATHA'S KIND HEART

Hiawatha threw down his bow and arrow. He waved to the squirrels to show them that he would not shoot their baby.

The baby squirrel came down the tree. All three squirrels offered to share their nuts with Hiawatha.

Kindness and friendship are the themes that inspire *Hiawatha's Kind Heart* (Volume 15). Hiawatha's dream of becoming an Indian brave is fulfilled, but through different methods than he originally planned! This story will help your child:

—recognize and identify animal pictures and names.

—learn the importance of kindness to animals and extend this idea to include people.

—recall details of the story and summarize the main idea.

—associate the /h/ sound with the letter *h*.

Reading *Hiawatha's Kind Heart*

Reading to Your Younger Child Read directly through the book with your child. Pause only long enough to identify the characters in the pictures and call them by name. On subsequent readings, use the pictures and text to help your child learn more about the animals. Where does each animal live? What does each animal eat? What are some of the activities each animal does? Talk about the kindnesses displayed by Hiawatha toward each animal and how the animals returned the favors.

Your Beginning Reader Reads to You Have your child read the story aloud to you. Patiently help him or her with difficult or unfamiliar word pronunciations. Encourage your child to read with the flow of the language, smoothly and evenly. Point out that where commas and periods appear are good places to pause for a breath. Your child should learn to plan ahead to breathe at these points.

Developing Reading Skills

Building Comprehension

Below are questions you may ask your child to bring out the main idea and details of the story. Permit your child to leaf through the book to look for clues or hints in the pictures and text.
1. What were Hiawatha's plans at the start of the story? Did he carry out his plans as he expected?
2. What kind of food did Hiawatha bring home to his mother and the chief?
3. Why did the chief think Hiawatha was wise? Do you think he was wise?
4. Why was Hiawatha proud of himself at the end?
5. Do you have a kind heart like Hiawatha? Give some examples of how you have been kind to animals and to people.

Expanding Vocabulary

Open the book to the first two pages and read the sentences aloud. Ask your child to point out words that name people (Hiawatha, braves, chief), places (town, forest), and things (food). You might want to identify these naming words as nouns. Go through the book with your child and have her or him find other words that name people. Go through the book again looking for places, and yet again looking for things. Later you may want to open the book randomly, point to a naming word, and ask your child to tell what category it belongs to—people, places, or things.

Fun with Phonics

Open the book to the first two pages. Point out and pronounce these words with your child: *Hiawatha, hard, hunt.* Tell your child that all these words begin with the letter *h* and this letter has the /h/ sound. Go through the book together looking for more words that begin with this letter and sound.

Fun-to-Read Activities

Dramatization Your child will have great fun moving and acting like the different animals in the story. Have your child act scared, as when the animals first saw Hiawatha. Then ask your child to show how each animal might show kindness toward a person who is kind to them.

Fun-to-Read Library

Compare Hiawatha's kindness to the animals with the nephews' kindness in *Wise Grandma Duck* (Volume 10) and with the friends' kindness in *Pooh Plans a Party* (Volume 18).

LI'L WOLF SAVES THE DAY

"But Li'l Wolf is our friend!" said Practical.

"He worked hard to get ready for the fair!" said Fifer.

"And he helped us to get ready, too," said Fiddler.

"Only pigs are allowed," said the guard. "And he is not a pig. He cannot come in."

"Well, then we won't go in either," said Practical.

"But you must!" cried Li'l Wolf. "If you don't, who will tell me about the fair afterward?" Then sadly Li'l Wolf walked away from the fair.

Li'l Wolf Saves the Day (Volume 16) tells of four friends who support each other, even though one of them is very different from the others. At the right time, Li'l Wolf sees to it that his friends and his father are protected. This story will help your child:

—understand and sympathize with the individual who is excluded because he or she is different.

—realize that being different need not be a barrier to friendship.

—retell events in time-order sequence.

—associate the letter *a* with its long and short sounds.

Reading *Li'l Wolf Saves the Day*

Reading to Your Younger Child First read right through the story. Enjoy the jokes the pigs play on Big Bad Wolf and their final solution to the problem. During the next few readings, emphasize various feelings characters show through text and pictures. Focus on how Li'l Wolf feels when he is refused admittance to the fair. Point out that the guard refuses Li'l Wolf only because he is different; as it turns out, Li'l Wolf is a very good friend.

Your Beginning Reader Reads to You Let your child look at the pictures and gain a general idea of the story. Then listen as your child reads to you, and assist her or him in pronouncing difficult words. On subsequent readings, encourage your child to try to sound out the phonetically regular words and to pay attention to the shapes formed by the letters of those words that do not follow the normal sound rules.

Developing Reading Skills

Building Comprehension

After you have read the story together, ask your child to answer questions such as the following:

1. Why were the three pigs excited about the County Fair? What was Big Bad Wolf excited about?
2. How did each pig get ready for the fair? How did Li'l Wolf get ready?
3. Why wouldn't the guard let Li'l Wolf into the fairgrounds? Why did he change his mind later?
4. What are some important things we should remember about what it means to be a friend?

Finally, encourage your child to retell the whole story in the correct time-order sequence, using words such as *first*, *next*, *then*, and *last*.

Fun with Phonics

Use the following lists of words to introduce the two sounds associated with the letter *a*:

Long /a/, pronounced like the name of the letter itself:

| saves | day | bake | race | great |

Short /a/, pronounced as in *at*:

| sack | ran | shack | catch |

Point out that words with the short /a/ sound do not have other vowels, but are surrounded by consonant letters. The long /a/ sound usually requires another vowel in the word, most commonly an *e*, to stretch out the sound. Look through the story for other examples of both sounds. Say the words aloud and talk about how they are constructed. You should find the following long /a/ words: *make*, *gate*, *made*, and *today*. Short /a/ words will include *can*, *can't*, *trap*, *bad*, *that*, and *fast*.

Fun-to-Read Activities

Dramatization Ask your child to pretend to be each of the three pigs and act as they did when they were preparing for the fair. Then ask your child to act as each of the wolves did as they prepared for the fair. Refer to the illustrations to help your child develop ideas for the characterizations.

Physical Fitness Have your child and a friend practice for a sack race and for a three-legged race. Select a large open space and a soft surface to prevent injuries from falling or bumping into things.

Fun-to-Read Library

Read about another kind of race in *Goofy's Big Race* (Volume 4). Compare the wolves in this story with the one in *Donald Cries "Wolf!"* (Volume 14). Compare Fiddler Pig and Fifer Pig practicing for the race with Daisy's preparation in *Donald Learns a Lesson* (Volume 17).

DONALD LEARNS A LESSON

At last Donald got back to Daisy's house. There stood Daisy. And she looked fresh as a daisy!

But Donald looked very tired. "Daisy, you won, fair and square," he said sadly. "I was not ready for this race. And you were!"

"I guess—" said Huey.
"—it pays—" said Dewey.
"—to be prepared!" shouted Louie.
"Yes," said Donald, "it certainly does!"

Imagine a fitness contest between Donald Duck and Daisy! In *Donald Learns a Lesson* (Volume 17), poor Donald is out-jumped and out-pedaled by the physically fit Daisy. Donald finally admits that Daisy was far better prepared for the contest than he was. This story will help your child:

—recognize the importance of eating right and exercising as part of a physical fitness program.

—learn the value of being prepared.

—add number words to the reading vocabulary.

—associate the /l/ sound with the letter *l*.

Reading *Donald Learns a Lesson*

Reading to Your Younger Child Before you read the story to your child, allow him or her to gain some familiarity with the characters and events by leafing quickly through the book. As you read, ask what might be happening in the picture on each page before you reveal the text on that page. After you are done, discuss whether your child had correctly interpreted the pictures (drawn the correct conclusions). Ask your child to describe Donald's feelings at the beginning of the story and at the end. How and why did these feelings change? What lesson did Donald learn?

Your Beginning Reader Reads to You After allowing your child a few quiet moments to examine the book, have her or him read you the story straight through. Assist with difficult words, but encourage your child to read for the meaning of the story. On subsequent readings, have your child take the time to attempt to read the unfamiliar words whose meanings may be inferred from the context. Discuss Donald's feelings and the lesson he learned as noted above.

Developing Reading Skills

Building Comprehension

Ask questions to help your child draw conclusions about the story. Permit him or her to refer to the book to clarify details or support theories. Some suggested questions are:

1. What was Donald dreaming about when the story began? How can you tell from the picture that he was dreaming?
2. How did Daisy keep fit and strong?
3. Was Donald as fit as Daisy? How can you tell?
4. What were the two parts of the contest? Who won each part?
5. What lesson did you learn from the story? Can you think of times when you should be prepared?

Expanding Vocabulary

Help your child find and read the following number words in the story: *one, two, three, four, five*. Write each word on an index card. On a second set of cards, have your child draw, or cut and paste, one to five objects. Show your child the correct way to write the numerals 1, 2, 3, 4, and 5 on a third set of cards. Mix all three sets of cards and then have your child find the matching triples.

For children who are more advanced, expand the activity to include numbers of objects, number words, and numerals 6 through 10.

Fun with Phonics

Read the following words with your child: *learn, lesson, look, listen, laugh*. Show your child that each of these words begins with the /l/ sound, which is spelled with the letter *l*. You may wish to have older children look for this sound and letter in the middle or at the end of words such as *Donald, sailing, rolled, trampoline*, and *all*.

Fun-to-Read Activities

Physical Fitness Encourage your child to make an exercise chart to keep track of practice sessions. Suggest suitable exercises and help her or him set reasonable goals. Many children will enjoy attending a local track meet or joining a children's exercise class, if available.

Fun-to-Read Library

Read about another kind of race in *Goofy's Big Race* (Volume 4). Contrast Daisy's preparation with that of Fiddler Pig, Fifer Pig, and Li'l Wolf in *Li'l Wolf Saves the Day* (Volume 16).

POOH PLANS A PARTY

All his friends were there. "Surprise!" they shouted. "Happy birthday, Eeyore! Surprise! Surprise!"

Eeyore was so happy that he did not know what to say.

Soon Christopher Robin came with cake and ice cream. Everyone sang and laughed, except for Eeyore. He almost smiled, though. And everyone wished Eeyore a happy birthday all over again.

Poor Eeyore thinks that all of his friends have turned away from him when no one will stop to talk. But as the reader of *Pooh Plans a Party* (Volume 18) knows, they are all on their way to get something to share with Eeyore at his surprise birthday party. This story will help your child:

—learn the importance of sharing.

—recall details and specific events.

—add more action verbs to the reading vocabulary.

—associate the short /e/ and long /e/ sounds with the letter *e*.

Reading *Pooh Plans a Party*

Reading to Your Younger Child As you read, help your child identify the characters from the pictures. Discuss what they brought to the party and how each item was shared. Ask your child to describe the party in her or his own words.

Your Beginning Reader Reads to You Before your child starts, it may be useful to identify each character. Write the names *Pooh, Kanga, Roo, Piglet, Eeyore, Gopher, Rabbit,* and *Christopher Robin* on index cards. Look at the pictures, and have your child select the correct name cards for the characters and say the names aloud. This exercise will help your child sail smoothly through the story as he or she reads to you. Discuss the details of the story with your child.

Developing Reading Skills

Building Comprehension

Pose questions to aid your child in understanding the theme of the story:
1. How did Eeyore feel about not knowing when his birthday is?
2. Why did Piglet think that Pooh was a clever bear?
3. How did Eeyore feel when everybody hurried off? How did he feel when he got home and saw all his friends?
4. Do you think Eeyore liked his birthday party?
5. Why did Pooh feel so warm and happy inside?
6. Can you think of something you shared, and did sharing it make you feel the way Pooh felt?

Expanding Vocabulary

The writer used action verbs that describe how the animals moved: *skipped, ran, hopped, bounced.* Read them and have your child locate and identify more descriptive action verbs. You may write these words on index cards and use them as reading flash cards.

Fun with Phonics

Read these words to familiarize your child with two sounds associated with the letter *e.*

Long /e/, pronounced like the name of the letter itself:

Eeyore	cheer	see	be

Short /e/, pronounced as in *get:*

when	then	went	red

Point out that words with the short /e/ sound do not have other vowels, but are surrounded by consonant sounds. The long /e/ is usually accompanied by another *e.* Look through the story again and have your child point out other examples of both sounds. Encourage your child to say the words aloud to be certain that they have been placed in the right category. Other words with long /e/ sounds you can find are: *he, need, we, bees, keep.* Among other words with short /e/ sounds are: *get, kept, doorstep.*

Fun-to-Read Activities

Dramatization Use the action flash cards from the vocabulary activity to play a game with your child. Put the cards facedown. Have your child select one card and, without letting you see it, act out how an animal would do the action on the card. You should guess what the animal is doing (hopping, bouncing, trotting) and name the animal.

Fun-to-Read Library

Read about another birthday that almost didn't get celebrated, in *Wendy's Adventure in Never Land* (Volume 9). Compare the friends' kindness to Eeyore with the kind deeds in *Wise Grandma Duck* (Volume 10) and *Hiawatha's Kind Heart* (Volume 15).